THE SHAPE OF THE STARS

By
Bob Devine

MOODY PRESS
CHICAGO

© 1977, by
The MOODY BIBLE INSTITUTE
OF CHICAGO

Second Printing, 1978

Library of Congress Cataloging in Publication Data

Devine, Bob
  The shape of the stars.

  (God in Creation series)
  SUMMARY: Explanation of five scientific phenomena which demonstrate God's involvement in
    the creation of the universe.
  1. Creation—Juvenile literature. [1. Creation
2. Science] I. Title. II. Series.
BS651.D49   212   77-9982
ISBN 0-8024-7896-4

Printed in the United States of America

CONTENTS

Chapter	Page
1. The Shape of the Stars	5
2. The Bluebird's Musical Heritage	11
3. The Snake with Heat-seeking Sensors	17
4. The Heart's Electric Generator	23
5. A Paint Factory in the Woods	29

1
The Shape of the Stars

In a day when we live better because of many scientific achievements, can the Bible be relied upon to tell us the truth about science? Many honest people are asking this question. The best way to solve the mystery is to investigate the claims of the Bible alongside true, factual science.

Nearly thirty-five hundred years ago, Moses wrote about the sun, moon, and stars, claiming that God had spoken to him about them. Genesis 1:14 says: "And God said, Let there be *lights* in the firmament of the heaven to divide the *day* from the *night;* and let them be for *signs*, and for *seasons,* and for *days,* and *years.*" Let's examine this verse and see if there are any scientific contradictions. First, Moses wrote of the "lights in the firmament of the heaven to divide the *day* from the *night.*" It's quite obvious he was speaking of the sun and moon. Verse 16 speaks of "two great lights; the greater light to rule the day, and the lesser light to rule the night." Certainly there is no contradition here. Nowhere does the Bible say the moon gives off its own light. We know the moon reflects the sun. This is one of the reasons why Moses called the moon the "lesser light."

The "lights" were also placed in the heavens to be a *sign* to mankind. There are numerous meanings to this portion of the verse, but one scientific meaning could be applied to the North Star, known as Polaris. So long as the sky is clear, the North Star is always visible. We know it has been a compass to the pilot, hunter, astronaut, and adventurer. It's a *sign* to those who are lost and easily points them to the direction north. All you need to do is find the two stars in the lip of the Big Dipper. Nearby, you'll see the Little Dipper. Find the last star in the handle of the Little Dipper. Now draw a line from the two stars in the lip of the Big Dipper to the last star in the handle of the Little Dipper. This points toward true north. Again, true science has no argument with the Bible when it says the "lights in the firmament of the heaven . . . [were] for *signs*."

Perhaps one of the most remarkable portions of Genesis 1:14 is: "Lights in the firmament of the heaven . . . [are] for *seasons*" (italics added). Many times in Scripture this refers to the moon marking the beginning of Jewish religious festivals or seasons. But another meaning is very evident from Scripture. Genesis 8:22 states, "While the earth remaineth, seed time and harvest, . . . summer and winter . . . shall not cease." This verse speaks of the four seasons, and it is a scientific fact that constellations of stars announce the four seasons. Here's how it works.

The five stars of the constellation Orion are only visible during the winter months of December, January, and February. This is also true of the constellation Canis Major, or the Great Dog. Therefore, if you didn't have a calendar and couldn't observe the weather but could only see the sky, you would know it was the winter season by these two constellations. People in the northern hemisphere only see these stars in the winter months because the earth is revolving around the sun, and these constellations come into view in the night sky.

As planet earth continues its orbit, the seasons change and so do the constellations. Orion and the Great Dog disappear from our view in the night sky, and the spring constellations make their debut. During the months of March, April, and May, any clear night in the northern hemisphere reveals the beauty of Leo the Lion, a constellation of seventeen stars in the shape of a roaring lion. The eight stars of Crater look like a water goblet. These are the welcomed constellations of springtime.

As the earth continues in its yearly orbit of the sun, we soon lose these clusters of stars, only to find new ones as summer comes. One of the most exciting constellations is Scorpius, a seventeen star configuration of a scorpion, tail and all. Sagittarius appears also during the summer months of June, July, and August. Its thirteen stars resemble a horse. But as the earth speeds along in its orbit of the sun, we soon lose these summer stars and notice some new ones in the autumn months of September, October, and November. The famous eight stars of the constellation Aquarius sparkle in the crisp night air, as do the four lights of Capricornus. These are known as autumn constellations. Then it won't be long until we see Orion and the Great Dog again, for the earth will just about have completed its orbit of the sun. Again, true science has no argument with the Bible. Moses was right when he said God put the "lights in the firmament of the heaven . . . for seasons."

Finally, the moon changes its phases gradually

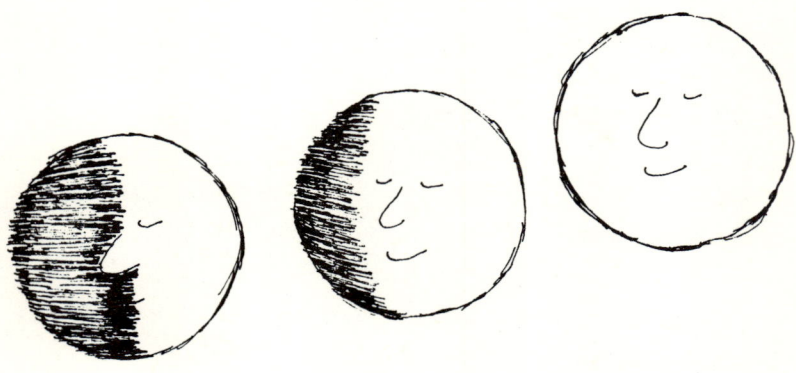

from day to day, clearly indicating that God put the "lights in the firmament of the heaven . . . for *days*." We know the earth makes its revolution of the sun in 365 days; therefore, God put the "lights in the firmament of the heaven . . . for . . . *years*."

Genesis 1:14 speaks loud and clear and says that true, factual science does not contradict the Bible. It's rather exciting to see that a thirty-five hundred-year-old Bible verse is still absolutely accurate and scientifically dependable. Since this verse is positively true, what does it say for the rest of Scripture? Second Timothy 3:16 (TLB) says, "The whole Bible was given to us by inspiration from God and is useful to teach us what is true."

2
The Bluebird's Musical Heritage

America's early settlers in Plymouth Colony referred to the eastern bluebird as the "blue robin." Henry David Thoreau, a naturalist as well as an author, spoke of this charming songster as one who "carries the sky on its back." The male bluebird is typically more colorful. With his handsome orange breast and bright blue back and head, it is understandable why the pilgrims called him the "blue robin." His pretty wife's colors are more subdued. Her blue is not as bright, and her breast is more gray than orange.

The five-syllable song of the eastern bluebird sounds like "cheer cheerful charmer." It's a gentle "chur-wi" tone. Always willing to brighten the day with a song, the bluebird even sings while flying. New York and Missouri have chosen this blue chorister as their state bird. But because of the use of pesticides in most orchards, the bluebird has left the flower paradise for other nesting sites. This may account for the alarming drop in the bluebird population in the United States. An overabundance of starlings and cowbirds, who rob the bluebird's nest, is also responsible.

Mr. and Mrs. Bluebird are early migrators, often arriving in the northern states in February or March. The late John Burroughs, another American naturalist, wrote, "In New York and New England the sap starts up the sugar maple the very day the bluebird arrives, and sugar making begins forthwith."

Often the bluebirds will build their nest in a hollow tree or maybe in a hole hammered out by a drumming woodpecker. In the nest, Mrs. Bluebird is camouflaged more perfectly than her mate. She lays four or five bluish white eggs and incubates them for about two weeks at a temperature of ninety-three degrees Fahrenheit (fifty-four degrees centigrade).

She pulls a patch of feathers from her abdomen, allowing the warm blood vessels that lie close to the surface of her skin to keep the eggs warm. This area on her body is called the "brood patch." Ninety-three degrees of constant heat is transferred from this patch to the eggs to provide good incubation. Who set her thermostat, one wonders. Food is important during this time to provide energy, which is transferred into body heat for the eggs. When the eggs hatch, Mr.

and Mrs. Bluebird work together as a team to raise their constantly hungry family.

Several years ago, an ornithologist at Cornell University in Ithaca, New York, gathered two eastern bluebird eggs from a nest box and incubated them in a laboratory. In two weeks he had a job on his hands: feeding a couple of hungry bluebirds. Kept in a warm, nestlike environment, the two fledglings were fed a blended mixture of cottage cheese, fruit, vitamins, antibiotics, earthworms, and chick starter. They grew well on this diet. The little speckle-chested birds were kept in an artificially lighted, soundproof cage, never once getting a glimpse of another bird—much less a bluebird. They never heard the warbling sound of their parents' song.

When they were six months old and full-grown, an experiment was performed to determine how the birds learn their call. Thus far they hadn't sung a note. Recorded songs of various birds were played to the two bluebirds, but very little interest was shown. The ornithologist wondered what would happen if he played the recording of an eastern bluebird. When he did, the birds came alive, responding strongly to the song and soon joining in the melody with their "cheer cheerful charmer." It's interesting to note that they wouldn't sing when they heard the recorded sounds of other birds. It was their own kind that awakened their musical interests. Why was this so?

It's awesome to realize that these birds never saw their parents and were never once instructed as to which song to sing. But they chose the melody of the eastern bluebird. Which do you credit: heredity or environment? Both have a part, but it is mostly heredity. The song of the eastern bluebird was determined by genetics. Before the eggs hatched, the eastern bluebird's unique sound was programmed into the brains of both the little birds. But it took an outside stimulus—a recording of their native song—to trigger the memory section of their little computers. Amazing, isn't it? Is it accidental? The Cornell experiment proved that heredity was the chief determining factor in the bluebird's song.

Has the blue bird ever had a different song? If so, what could have caused it to change? Since the song is passed on to the young through genes and chromosomes, science concludes that environment cannot change the eastern bluebird's song. What does this say about the two birds' parents and the thousands and millions of generations that preceded them? Does it speak of order or chaos? Was God involved in the genetic makeup of the eastern bluebird? If not, how else can we scientifically explain this phenomenon?

Some might speculate that the eastern bluebird interbred with other birds. But this has never been observed by an ornithologist. It might be done artificially in the laboratory, but never in the wild. Scientists can force a genetic change by interbreeding, but this goes against the bird's will. In the wild, scientists note that "birds of a feather flock together," refusing to crossbreed. Therefore, the bluebird genes had to be in this orange and blue bird from the beginning. Observable science and the Bible never contradict one another. Genesis 1:21 states that "God created . . . every winged fowl after his kind: and God saw that it was good."

3
The Snake with Heat-Seeking Sensors

A rattlesnake measures heat more accurately than most thermometers known to man today. A change of .002 degrees centigrade, two thousandths of a degree, is easily detectable. Most people don't quibble about one degree, much less a percentage of a degree. If you care to chance it, a rattler is able to detect the heat radiated from the human hand held a foot away. What makes this pit viper so sensitive to warmth that it can follow the heat trail of a small animal through underbrush after the animal is completely out of sight? The answer is one-eighth inch wide (3 millimeters) and one-quarter inch deep (6 millimeters). These are the dimensions of the rattlesnake's two heat-sensitive pits located between his eyes and nostrils.

Old Dead Eye, the rattler, slithers out of his den after dark and samples the night air with his forked tongue. Friendly breezes carry the scent of a meadow mouse scurrying about for food. As the snake pulls his tongue back in his mouth, his taste buds transfer to his brain the message that food is near. Coiled and ready for action in the pitch-black night, Old Dead Eye turns his head until his heat-sensitive pits pick up a strong amount of heat radiation. The rattler has zeroed in on the mouse's trail by the heat left in its footprints. Now within striking distance, the reptile sweeps his head back and forth, determining the size of the rodent from the width of the heat radiation. This information is sent immediately to the snake's brain and Old Dead Eye's computer tells him precisely how far the mouse is from him so he can adjust his striking distance. With two hundred ball-and-socket joints in his backbone, Old Dead Eye is very flexible. He can wheel and deal quickly and pack a sudden deathblow.

Do you have any idea how the rattlesnake got his heat-detecting pits? What caused his brain to compute and decipher the message from his pits?

The rattlesnake has two hollow hypodermiclike fangs in his top jaw that fold back against the roof of his mouth when not in use. However, when he becomes angry and opens his yawning crevice wide, the two fangs snap out, ready for action. An attached gland contracts and pumps deadly venom through the hollow fangs into the victim.

Dr. Noble of the American Museum of Natural History spent considerable time studying rattlesnakes. He discovered the reptile's heat-sensitive pits by an experiment. He blindfolded a rattler by taping adhesive over each eye. Would the snake be able to strike accurately? Surely it couldn't see! Next Dr. Noble focused an electric light bulb at its head and—zapp! When the heat from the bulb reached the sensitive pits, the rattler struck right on target. Then Dr. Noble covered the left pit and aimed the light on it, not allowing any of the heat to strike the right pit. The snake did not react. Focusing the heat from the lamp on the uncovered right pit, the blindfolded snake hit its target.

Dr. Noble proved the rattlesnake didn't need to see his target in order to hit it. The thermostatic pits on the snake's head were perfect sensors for the heat, and his brain calculated the accurate distance. If the heat appeared stronger in the right pit, the rattler swung right when striking, zeroing in on his target. This logically explains why the rattlesnake is so successful a hunter at night. Obviously his eyes are useful during the day and night for navigation, but he doesn't need them to find his food. He operates with heat-sensitive pits.

How did the rattlesnake develop his sophisticated heat-sensing equipment? Or, did he? Evolution claims it was through trial and error over millions of years, and that the rattlesnake finally perfected his heat-homing device by natural selection. But is this scientific? Evolutionary teaching claims so, but let's double-check to make sure.

The Sidewinder Guided Missile, made for warfare, uses the same heat-sensing principle as a rattlesnake. The heat given off by a high-flying jet plane is like a magnet to the Sidewinder Missile when released from its pad. It electronically locks onto the heat path of the plane's jet stream and zeroes in for the kill. How similar to the rattlesnake's pit-detection system. Who copied from whom?

Who is more intelligent: the evolutionary system or modern scientist? Be careful! According to evolution,

isn't man the highest form of life and at the top of the ladder? This intelligent man has designed and developed the Sidewinder Guided Missile, copying its basic design after the rattlesnake's guidance system. Yet evolution teaches that the rattlesnake evolved over millions of years, having no designer and builder, even though it is superior to the missile.

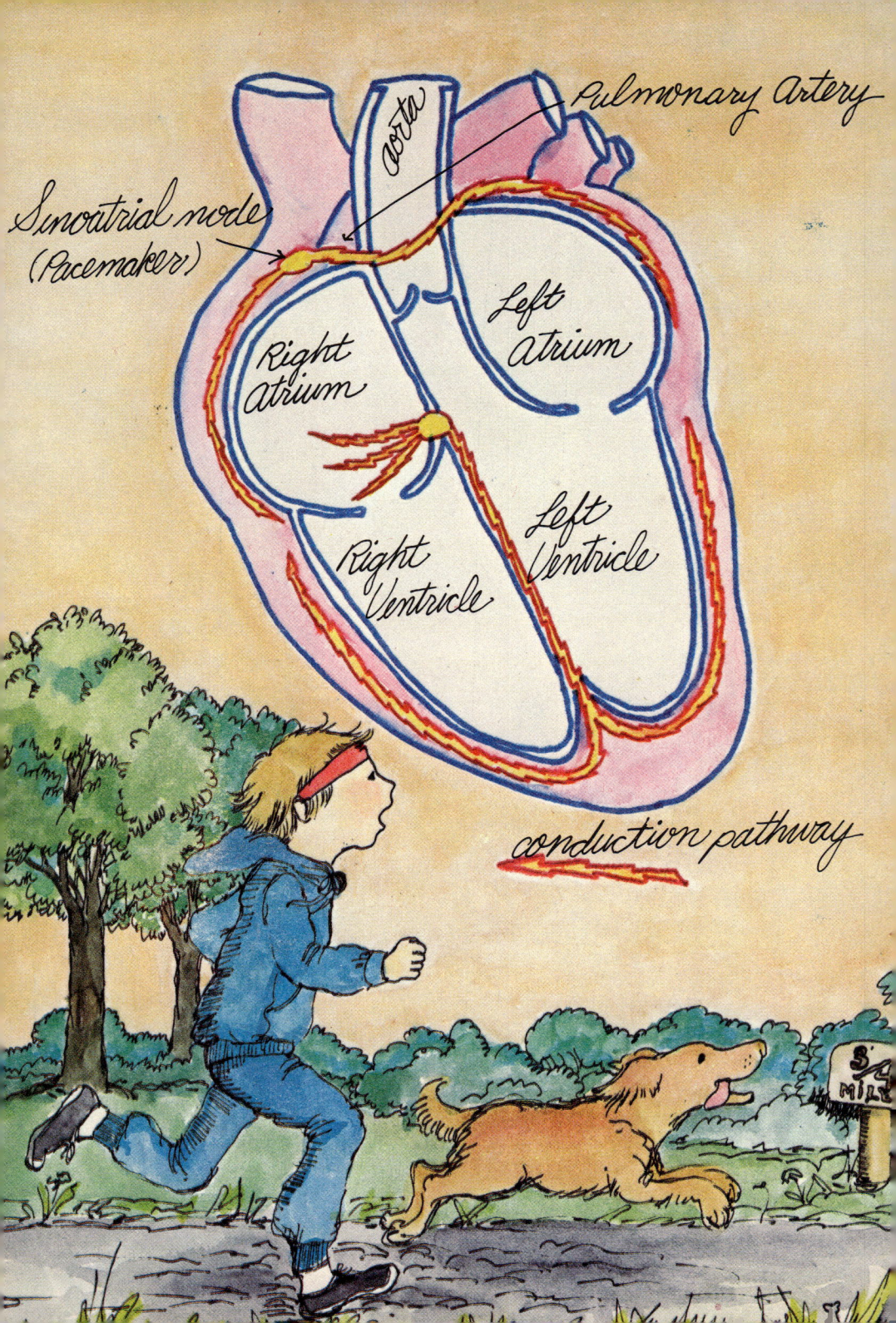

4
The Heart's Electric Generator

Did you know your heart operates by electricity? This may not come as a surprise to you, for most pumps in our modern-day world run on at least 110 volts. The human heart, however, is far more conservative with its use of energy, for it operates on only 1 volt of D.C. electricity! That sounds like flashlight power. But there's really no need to worry about your "battery" running low, because you don't have one. What you have is far more advanced, dependable, and sophisticated. It's known as the sinoatrial node, more modern than tomorrow's scientific discovery, yet as old as man himself. Doctors speak of this electrical generator as the S. A. Node. Located in the heart it is about the size of a marble. Heart specialists are amazed at this highly technical source of power that just keeps on functioning nonstop night and day, usually for at least seventy years.

Every time you feel your heart beat, your two ventricles are pumping blood throughout your body. But what causes them to pump? The same force that makes any pump operate: electricity! Just one volt of it, almost what you would find in a flashlight battery. Only your "battery" is much smaller and billions of times more efficient than a flashlight battery.

Let's form a picture in our minds of what this represents. The left and right ventricles are comparable to two pumps. Leading to them are nerve pathways, which are similar to electrical wires. The S.A. Node is the electrical generator. Therefore, we have a voltage supply attached to a load (the ventricles) by a network of nerves. As the voltage from the S.A. Node enters the ventricles, the voltage shocks the ventricles and causes them to contract, thus pumping blood.

But all this would be of no value if the S.A. Node supplied a continuous, unbroken flow of electricity to the ventricles. The S.A. Node must turn off and then on again, off and on, off and on. This allows the ventricles to squeeze and release, squeeze and release, in a pumping action. In order to operate this way, the voltage to the ventricles must be turned on and off at the S.A. Node. Within this marble-sized electrical generator is a highly sophisticated electronic switch that turns the voltage on and off on a regulated basis. Many times, though, the heartbeat quickens. This change is controlled by the central nervous system, which, in turn, is controlled by the brain.

It's obvious that all generators need either force or fuel to operate. The fuel for the S.A. Node is in the form of oxygen. Without this well-known gas, the human body would cease to function. The S.A. Node could not produce its one volt of electricity, thereby shutting down the circulatory system. This would trigger a critical energy crisis. The S.A. Node receives its fresh oxygen supply from the blood. An abundant supply of rich oxygen is added to the blood in the lungs, which shows the importance of keeping our lungs clean.

The S.A. Node provides the electricity that operates the ventricles which pump seventy times a minute, one hundred thousand times a day, sending life-giving blood through one hundred thousand miles of blood vessels in your body night and day without failure for about seventy years. Now and then an S.A. Node breaks down. Cardiologists have developed a man-made S.A. Node called the artificial pacemaker, which basically does the job of the defective S.A. Node and keeps the patient alive.

Electrical generating plants are carefully designed and built by brilliant scientists. What does this say for the S.A. Node? Doctors say it exceeds the efficiency of the best generators man can design. Yet what man has designed is great! Think for a moment of who planned and built the S.A. Node! He would be greater, wouldn't He? Or do we credit mother nature for this, or perhaps evolution? To say evolution is responsible for the heart's electrical generator is to say the best generators designed by man also evolved, because they are inferior to the S.A. Node. A design always comes from a designer, and the Lord Jesus Christ is the master Designer of the sinoatrial node. Wouldn't it be great to tie into His kind of power!

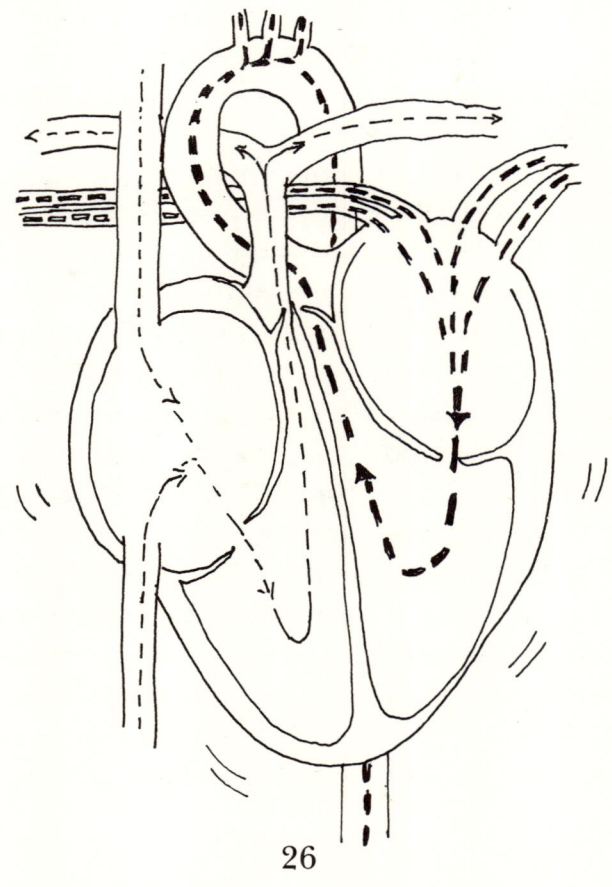

5

A Paint Factory in the Woods

What is more beautiful than a hillside of sugar maple trees in autumn? The brilliant splashes of red, orange, and yellow are almost breathtaking, and the greens of hemlock and spruce add a contrasting luster to the fall landscape. October is a time of unparalleled beauty in the countryside.

What causes leaves to change color? The most common answer autumn hikers give is: a frost! But a frost only damages the leaves, causing them to turn brown and fall. Cool weather does add to the beauty of the leaf color, but it isn't the cause. Surprisingly, the colors we see in the autumn leaves were really there all summer. The reason we didn't see them was that chlorophyll covered the colors. Chlorophyll is a combination of two Greek words: *chloros*, meaning "green," and *phyll* meaning "leaf." Lots of sunshine and carbon dioxide are vital in the manufacture of chlorophyll in leaves; so are two chemicals: nitrogen and magnesium. They enter the roots, flow up the trunk into the branches, and end their journey in the leaves.

Because there is abundant sunshine in the summertime, as much as fifteen hours a day, chlorophyll is produced in each leaf, covering up another process we don't see until autumn. Depending on the kind of tree, three different substances work in the summer to produce beautiful colors in the leaves. Sugar maples have carotene, an orange color. Some maples have anthocyanins, which make a red color. Tulip trees, birches, and elms have a lot of xanthophyll pigment that is yellow in color. Sweet gum trees have all three color pigments. During the good old summertime though, the lavish amounts of sunshine cause the chlorophyll to cover up the beautiful colors that are present.

Trees reproduce after their own genetic kind. Who placed the pigments in the tree's system? Did evolutionary processes accomplish this, or was it a higher intelligence?

When daylight hours become shorter, something amazing happens in the leaf. The change from fifteen hours of summer sun in late June to eleven and one-half hours a day in October flashes a signal to the leaf's stem. This three and one-half hour reduction in sunlight causes a thick, double layer of cork cells to form at the base of the leaf stem, blocking the flow of nitrogen and magnesium so necessary for the production of chlorophyll in the leaf. Within a few days, the green color fades because chlorophyll can no longer be produced in the leaf factory. Gradually the change becomes evident. The bright autumn hues that were present but hidden all summer can now be seen. The key to the color change is the shortened daylight hours which come in mid-October. They are also responsible for changing the snowshoe rabbit's fur from a camouflaging summer brown to winter white. The weasel and ptarmigan are likewise affected. Considering how plants and animals are affected by the length of daylight hours, does this indicate anything about orderliness in our universe? Trees near streetlights usually are late in turning color because the extra light is like added daylight hours, fooling the tree's sensitive system.

Fall colors are enchanced by sunny days and cool nights. The warm Indian summer days cause the leaves to produce sugar, which brightens the leaf's color, especially if it's red. If nights are cool, the leaves will not lose their sugar to transpiration. Transpiration is to plants what perspiration is to human beings.

Soon a mysterious wisp of autumn wind sways the branches of the sugar maples, and the rustle of falling leaves is heard. The leaf stem breaks off at the layer of cork cells that were formed because of the shortened daylight hours. Night falls on the forest of gorgeous maples. An owl hoots in a nearby butternut tree. Soon clouds cover the sky, and rain falls. Down come more autumn leaves. Now they can be raked into huge piles, shredded, and tilled into the garden. They'll greatly improve the quality of the soil.

Considering the intricate workings of a leaf factory, we must conclude that there is strong evidence for design. When we see scientific evidence of design and order, we conclude quite accurately that a designer was involved. This same Architect who causes color change in leaves can also make a great positive change in your life. The Bible tells it like it is. "Therefore, if anyone is *in Christ,* he is a new creation; the old has gone, the new has come!" (2 Corinthians 5:17, NIV, italics added).